AS A WISE MAN ONCE SAID...

Aharon Shemi
Danny Kerman

English: Tamar Berkowitz

KIVUNIM

AS A WISE MAN ONCE SAID...

Kivunim Publishing House Ltd.
Achim Trebes st. 3, Rehovot 76488,
Israel.

Kivunim Publishing House Ltd.
copyright © 1983 by
ISBN - 965-276-008-0
Printed in Israel

FOREWARD

There are two types of people in the world. There are those who quote a saying by Mark Twain, for instance, and pretend they made it up on the spot. And then there are those who make up a saying and give Mark Twain the credit (or the blame). We are among the second type. By the way, "we," as Mark Twain once said, "is something that can be said only by someone who has worms." The truth is, things aren't quite so simple. There are times when it is preferable "to quote" George Bernard Shaw, and there are others when it is best to rely on La Rochefoucauld, Voltaire, and the others. And in this matter we believe that the Duke of Norfolk was absolutely right when he said "Quotations, like long words, are a matter of luck." Even so, it seems it would be an error to credit the famous saying "The rich are like pigs; they are useful only after their death" to the Lubavitcher Rebbe. You could credit it to George Orwell, who specialized in pigs, or to Oscar Wilde, who specialized in life after death, although we should note, for the sake of the record, that this saying was authored this very minute.

Making up sayings, like making up jokes, is much easier than it seems at first. First of all, there are formulas. They almost all begin with "Life is." Or, as we opened our foreword, "There are two types of people..." And that reminds us that a wise man once said that there are two types of people -- those who divide people into two types, and those who don't. We also know someone who divides people like this: One group consists of herself, and the second of everyone else. To summarize briefly, we can make the following conclusions:

1. Somebody nevertheless makes sayings up.
2. Many people use them from time to time.
3. The lack of a book on this subject is an open pit which must be filled.*

The Authors

* The pit cannot be filled from its own digging. (Our Sages of Blessed Memory)

We should worry about making the world just, before worrying about teaching our children that justice pays.*

* In other words, we have a lot to worry about!

Fish and ducks live in water and die in wine.*

* Note to the author of this saying: so do bacteria.

Training is everything. The peach was once a bitter almond; cauliflower is nothing but cabbage with a college education.*

(Mark Twain)

* Ronald Reagan, for instance, was once a C-actor in B-movies.

Arguing with a woman is like reading a newspaper against a strong wind.*

(Oscar Wilde)

* A woman was once asked why women always take everything personally. "Who said so?" she answered, "I never do!"

Soap and education are not as sudden as a massacre, but they are more deadly in the long run.*

(Mark Twain)

* If you don't understand this saying, you should read the following story carefully:

The famous General Posh once met with the head of a cannibal tribe. He told him that in the F[
World War millions of men were killed.

"How did you manage to eat them all in time?" asked the surprised cannibal.

"In Europe," explained the general, "we don't eat our enemy."

"What, you kill just for the sake of it, and not for food?" exclaimed the cannibal, "How barbar[

Shrouds are made without pockets.*

* This information is intended for those of you who are wealth. So if you want to take it with you when you go, you should equip yourself in plenty of time, with checkbooks, suitcases, backpacks, etc. But just remember, they cost money too.

God is always on the side of the winning army.*
(Voltaire)

* Stalin never read Voltaire. Otherwise how could he have asked, "How many divisions has the Pope?"

A politician is a man who promises to build a bridge even where there is no river.*

* Or, in short, a politician is a man who promises.

If you fear loneliness, don't get married.*

* A nice saying, but that's not the only reason. Use this one only after you've run out of others.

In order to save your reputation, give in public and steal in secret.*

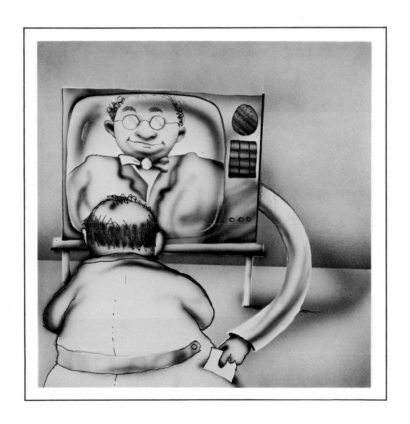

* This saying originally appeared as the title of a book on the fundamentals of public relations.

Experience is a school where you learn how stupid you were.*
(Henry Ford)

* The problem is, the diploma is received by your heirs.

Behind every successful man stands a surprised mother-in-law.*

* Even such a clever saying should not be taken at face value. We have seen men behind whom their mothers-in-law sit and even some behind whom a mother-in-law lies.

Money is like muck; not good unless it be spread.*
(Francis Bacon)

* On the other hand, it is also said that money has no smell. So let's see you try to run your life according to sayings.

In mathematics, as in democracy, the one derives its strength from the number of worthless figures behind it.*

* Even if 50,000 people say something's stupid, that's no proof that it isn't.

Liberty means responsibility. That is why most men dread it.*

(George Bernard Shaw)

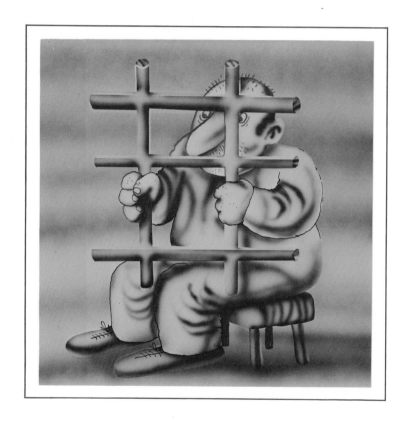

* And this is another explanation for the fact that such an amazing number of people get married.

A guest and a fish smell after three days.*
(Conrad Hilton)

* The similarity between them is that neither is aware of this, and the difference is that fish can be thrown out.

A radical is a man with both feet firmly planted in the air.*

(Franklin Roosevelt)

* From a message intended to be broadcast on Arbor Day.

A person will always sell his last robe if it means he can be rich.*
(Shalom Aleichem)

* There was a beggar who always said that if he were Rothschild he would be richer than Rothschild. "How's that?" people would wonder. "Because I would continue to beg."

Stinginess is also a form of income.*
(Oscar Wilde)

* On the other hand, better to be just a miser than also stingy miser.

We are all descendants of the ape, but on some it is more evident.*

(George Bernard Shaw)

* Where does a 3-ton gorilla sit? Wherever he wants to. (From the Gorilla Manual)

We can tolerate anything but the continuous success of others.*

(Stephen Leacock)

* ...and toothache: which is why we suffer doubly at the dentist's.

There is no feature used more by a politician than a poor memory.*

* His own and especially that of others.

A cynic is a man who when he smells flowers looks for a funeral.*

* George Bernard Shaw did not like receiving flowers.
"Do you hate flowers?" he was asked.
"I like children, too, but I don't trim their heads and stick them in a vase!"

God loves fools. Otherwise why would he have made so many?*

* You can use this saying freely. We haven't yet met a person who was offended by it.

A classic is something that everybody wants to have read and nobody wants to read.*

(Mark Twain)

* A classic saying.

Pancakes in a dream are a dream and not pancakes.*

(Shalom Aleichem)

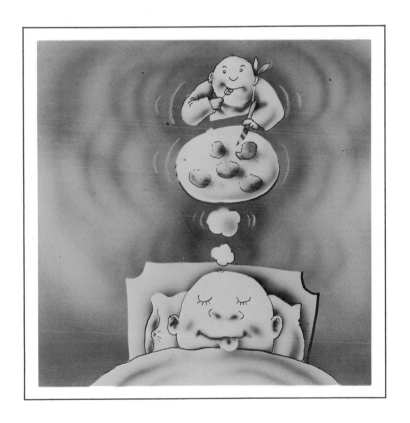

* Just like income tax is tax and not income.

A pessimist is an optimist who tried to put his theory into practice.*

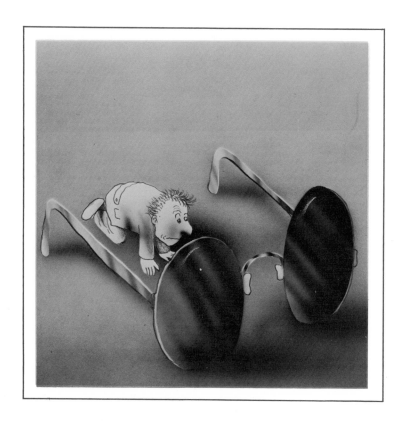

* And an optometrist is a person who fits glasses for those with vision problems. (See also, "long words are a matter of luck".)

Marriage is an attempt to solve problems together that would not even exist if you were alone.*

* In one town there were two men. One was very rich; he traveled in a splendid carriage, pulled by a pair of grand horses. The other, poor, traveled in a wagon pulled by a skinny mare. "And what will you do if your wagon gets stuck in the mud?" the rich man jeered. "That mare will never get you out."

"What you fail to understand, " answered the poor man, "is that this mare will also never get me into the mud."

There is no man more empty than he who is full of himself.*
(Confucius)

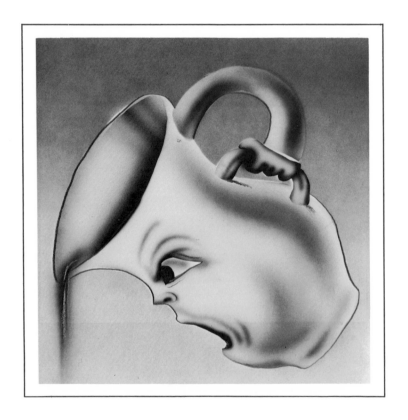

* Have you noticed, for instance, that the most boring people are those who begin every sentence with the word "I"?

You have nothing more precious than to hide the fact that you haven't a cent in your pocket.*

(Anthony Quinn)

* One must take into account that most proverbs were written by the have-nots.
Those who do have money have no time for such nonsense.

"We" is something that can be said only by a person who has worms.*

(Mark Twain)

* Every time that someone says "we", try to tell him this. It works wonderfully! We tried it.

An opinion is not made more correct just because somebody sacrifices himself for it.*

(Oscar Wilde)

* And here's the proof: every child today knows that the earth is flat and stationary and that the sun revolves around it.

The conscience of the politician is clean because it is hardly ever used.*

(Benjamin Disraeli)

* Conscience and humor have something in common -- they are both things that you have and others don't.

Only someone who falls in love with himself need not expect disappointment.* **
(Benjanim Franklin)

* If he doesn't snore.
** Of course, then he can't fall in love with the daughter of a millionaire.

Many people would like to be married, but not 24 hours a day.*

* The problem is that later they also want to be parents, but not 24 hours a day (dedicated to Daniella).

Two heads are better than one, especially with regard to asparagus.*

* In order to show he was right, a mayor once said to the Opposition leader, "It won't help you, we are ten heads here against one."
"If you like big numbers so much," replied his opponent, "why don't you say 20 legs?"

I'm not so young that I know everything.*

* A man has two high spots in his life: when he is 3, and when he is 18. At age 3 he knows the questions and at age 18 he knows all the answers. (Andre Maurois)

Put all your eggs in the one basket and
WATCH THAT BASKET.*
(Mark Twain)

* A hen is only an egg's way of making another egg. (Samuel Butler)

Long words are a matter of luck.*

* For instance, you need an etymologist to tell an entomologist from an econometrist, especially if you're hemeralopic.

There are two things that are infinite --
the universe and the stupidity of man.*

(Albert Einstein)

* And you can count on Einstein; he was always right, relatively.

Knowledge is what remains after you forget what you learned at school.*
(Albert Einstein)

* What's the difference between a fool and a madman? The fool thinks 2 times 2 is 5. The madman knows it's 4, but it drives him mad.

The world is made up of three types of people: those who can't be moved, those who can be moved, and those who move by themselves.*

* And there are those who say the world is made up of 3 things, but 2 of them are always out-of-order.

A man who seeks a woman who is good, wise and beautiful is actually looking for three women.*

(Oscar Wilde)

* What Oscar Wilde didn't understand - and perhaps couldn't - is that there's nothing wrong with three women.

When you bury a rich mother-in-law, don't skimp on expenses.*

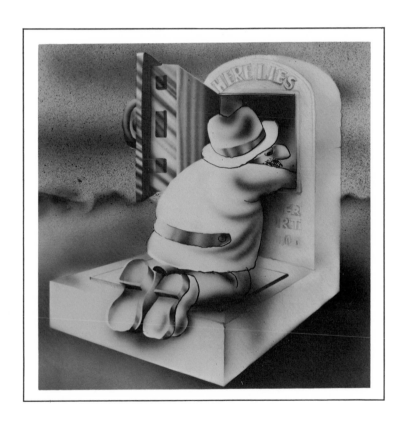

* Anyway, it's a tax deduction.

The university is a gathering place for knowledge. The new students bring a little with them; the graduates leave with none. And that's how the knowledge is gathered.*

* To prove it, try this saying on a university professor, and you'll be sure to see that he doesn't think it's funny.

If you want to get rid of someone, lend him some money.*

* The converse is even more certain: If you want to get rid of some money, lend it to someone.

Everything has a beginning, a middle, and an end, but not necessarily in that order.*

* Anyone who ever saw one of Godard's movies knows exactly what he meant.

Housecleaning, all in all, is moving dust from one place to another.*

* Just imagine how many days of work the inventor of this saying saved himself, and just imagine what his house looks like.

There are two solutions to every problem: the wrong one, and mine.*

(Thomas Alva Edison)

* For those who wish to use this saying, we have two suggestions:
1st suggestion: Be sure to say "two solutions"; if you say "three" or "four", you ruin the saying.
2nd suggestion: Don't eat heavy food before bed; it's not good for you.

People get married because the government can't be blamed for everything.*

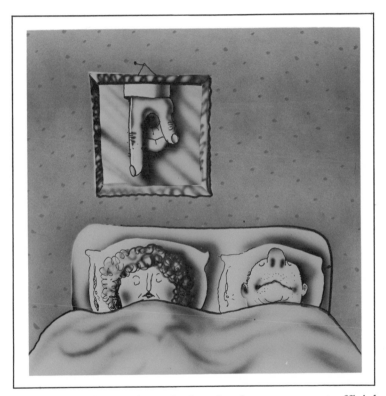

* If this book should fall, by chance, into the hands of a government official, we do not recommend that he use this saying too freely. For, despite this message, the government is, nevertheless, responsible for most things. You also have to take into account that most government officials are married.

Men use thought only to justify their wrongdoing, and words only to conceal their thoughts.*

(Voltaire)

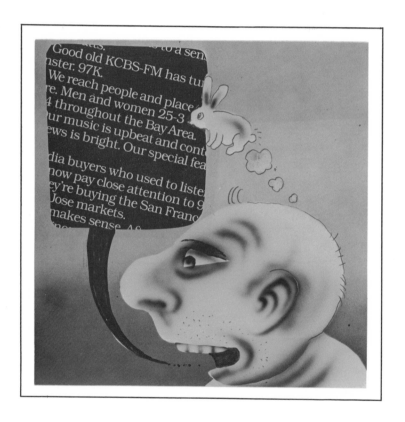

* This saying suited the period of Voltaire. At that time you could still say "men use thought" without being laughed at.

The mind is a marvelous thing -- it starts working when you get up in the morning and continues until you get to the office.*

* You may replace the word "office" with any other place of work.

There are some people who will do anything for money -- even good deeds.*

* There are. But not many.

A statesman thinks of the next generation, a politician of the next elections.*

* A politician who is also a statesman arranges for the next elections to be held in the next generation.

It is better to remain silent and be thought a fool than to open your mouth and prove it.*

* ------------------------

"You should always hear both sides" is a very wise saying that was invented before the phonograph record.*

* The record was invented by Emil Berliner at the end of the nineteenth century.

It were not best that we should all think alike; it is difference of opinion that makes horse-races.*

(Mark Twain)

* But if you want to have a horse race, you should also get some horses.

You shouldn't talk much about yourself in company -- once you've left the others wil do so anyway.*

* And for those who are left in the room, the accepted procedure is to count to 50 if you're on the ground floor, and to 30 on higher floors, before starting in. In a building with an elevator, you just have to send someone out to see if the rat's gone.

He who can, does. He who cannot, teaches. And he who can't teach, directs.*

(George Bernard Shaw)

* Anybody who tells you that mental work is harder than physical work is mistaken -- I know, I've done them both... (Mark Twain).